Lifesty of the Rich & FLATULENT

(FULL OF GAS)

Written by THELMA LaBacus   ILLUSTRATED BY V.G. MYERS

A

Publication

ISBN 0 - 9639812 - 2 - 6   Printed in U.S.A.

In the Garden

"SO HOW ARE MY LITTLE DARLINGS TODAY?"

On the Hunt

"THE DOGS HAVE LOST THE SCENT AGAIN."

In the Study

"I WOULDN'T LIGHT THAT RIGHT NOW, IF I WERE YOU, SIR".

At the Opera

On the Yacht

"I SAY OLD MAN. THERE SEEMS TO BE AN ILL WIND 'A BLOWIN'."

At the Auction

"SOLD!... AT A FRACTION OF THE VALUE, TO THE LONE BIDDER".

In the Library

Page 16

Golfing

"IT'S A GIMME! IT'S A GIMME!"

On the Polo Field

"NOW THAT'S A FAST POLO PONY."

On the Lawn

"NOW THAT'S A BIT OF A STINKY WICKET."

On the Courts

"I WIN!! TIME TO SWITCH COURTS!"

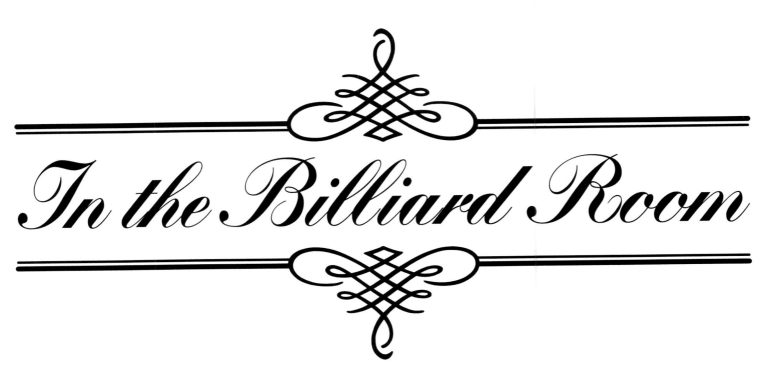

In the Billiard Room

"THAT SHOT STINKS."

On Safari

"WE GOTTA' STAY DOWNWIND IF WE'RE EVER GOING TO BAG ANY GAME."

In the Boardroom

"GENTLEMEN, WE HAVE NOW SURPASSED OUR EXPECTATIONS."

On the Veranda

"OH MY. I MUST HAVE THE VAPORS." "YES DEAR, I TRULY BELIEVE YOU DO."

On a Shopping Spree

"MAY I GET YOU A TINY BIT LARGER SIZE MADAME?"

In the Parlor

"RICH PEOPLE HAVE A CERTAIN AIR ABOUT THEM."

Crusin' in the Limo

"EXCUSE ME, BUT DO YOU HAPPEN TO HAVE A 'FAART EXTINGUISHER'?"

Jet Setting

"THIS IS FIRST CLASS! WHAT DO YOU MEAN THE WINDOWS DON'T OPEN?!"

At the Club's Pool

"ISN'T THAT THE CEO OF MR. BUBBLES?"

Gourmet Dining

"WILL THERE BE A NEED TO SNIFF THE CORK, SIR?"

Nanny Day at the Park

"PITY, THE OTHER CHILDREN WON'T PLAY WITH LITTLE LORD FARTLAROY."

Hot Air Ballooning

"ISN'T THIS A GAS?"

In the Oil Field

"...AND BILL HERE, MADE HIS FORTUNE IN OIL AND 'GAS'!"